College Basketball:
A Player's Perspective

By Chad Rykhoek & Teri Crisco

@chadunocinco

Copyright © 2019 Chad Rykhoek and Teri Crisco

All rights reserved

ISBN: 978-1-7339194-0-1

No part of this book may be reproduced, stored in a retrieval system, or transmitted in any form, or by any means whether by electronic, mechanical, photocopy, recording or otherwise, without the prior written permission of the copyright owner except in the case of a brief quotation embodied in a critical review and certain other noncommercial uses permitted by copyright law. For all other uses, requests for permission may be sent to the publisher, "Attention: Permissions Coordinator," at the following email address: cbbperspective@gmail.com.

I pray you find your purpose.

"Many are the plans in a person's heart, but it is God's purpose that prevails."
Proverbs 19:21

CONTENTS

Introduction 1
My Dream 4
My Growing Up Years 8
The College Recruiting Process 29
The Division 1 Basketball Experience: Freshman Year 33
Surgery Number One: Postseason and Summer after Freshman Year 38
Surgery Number Two: End of First Semester of Sophomore Year 40
Surgery Number Three: Second Semester of Sophomore Year 43
Surgery Number Four, Five, Six, and More 45
From Medical Exempt to Medical Release 47
The Transition from Student-Athlete to Student & College Graduation 48
What Now? What Next? 54
Moving on for a Master's Degree 55
Another Disappointing Injury and Setback 61
Surgery Number Seven 75
Back to Basketball for a Sixth-Year Comeback 78
The End of College Basketball in Pursuit of a Professional Career 80
Lessons Learned 85
What Is It Really Like to be a College Athlete? 89
Growth from Freshman Year to Senior Year 94
When it Comes to an End 96
The Mental Aspect 101
The Medical Aspect 102
In Retrospect 104
Regrets? 105
Different Personality Types 107
Advice for Young Athletes 109
Conclusion 110

Introduction
Everybody Has a Story to Tell

Everybody has a story to tell, tales of life experiences, both good and bad. Every individual's story is unique. No one else's story is the same as yours. I am no exception. My life's journey to date has been full of ups and downs, good days and bad days, excitement and sadness, problems and solutions, rejection and acceptance. I have a lot of memories to cherish as well as those I wish I could erase, dreams fulfilled and some yet to be achieved, expectations satisfied and some yet to be met. But I have very few regrets.

Life is not just a series of chance happenings. Luck does not play a part in this process called life, because the God who created the universe is in control. I believe He orchestrates things to happen according to His perfect plan and will for our lives. Knowing this gives me a peace that passes all understanding, no matter the circumstances. I trust God while walking on the path He has for me. God doesn't force anything on us. He gave each one of us free will. We make choices and decisions along the way that have a direct impact on us. We must always keep in mind the importance of asking God for wisdom and direction so that our choices and decisions line up with His will. Only when we choose to do what lines up with God's perfect plan does life become smoother and go more successfully, therefore making life a much happier journey.

I have always strived to make good choices. My personality includes being a perfectionist and a people pleaser. I have a strong sense of right versus wrong, and I try my best to consistently do what is right. I am easygoing, reserved, and quiet for the most part, which has often led to me being misunderstood. In high school, some teachers wouldn't give me an E for "excellent" in Conduct, because I didn't participate enough in class. I never did anything wrong and was an excellent student, but some teachers gave me only an S for "satisfactory." In the basketball realm, my cool, collected, non-aggressive personality was often misinterpreted as me being less than motivated or not working hard enough.

Things are not always as they seem. Looking at someone's life from the outside doesn't always yield a fair assessment of that person. You have to have walked in their shoes and lived what they have experienced to fully comprehend and understand what has brought people to where they are today, as their experiences would have played a significant part in making them who they are as an individual. Obviously, people would respond to circumstances very differently. But before you label or judge someone, it is important to be certain that you have all the facts and background information first.

An outsider looking in would think my life after high school has been a bust. If they simply looked at my bio and stats, they would conclude that my accomplishments have not been all that great. But, knowing what has happened behind the scenes over the course of those years would shed light and bring perspective on the situation to portray a true picture. With regard to basketball, I don't believe I was valued or utilized fully at the college level, and I'll explain more later on.

There are people who probably have a more riveting story to tell, but I want to share my story with the hope that it will be an encouragement and inspiration to all who read it. My prayer is that what God has allowed me to walk through so far on this journey called life and the lessons I have learned along the way will help someone else walk courageously, by faith, and persevere.

1

My Dream

My dream from a very young age was to play basketball in college at the highest level, do well, and then go on to play in the NBA. Given my height (7 feet), that was a very real possibility. Combined with the gifts and talents God blessed me with, it seemed as though my dream could become a reality.

People always wonder what it is like to be 7 feet tall. For me, it is simply normal, and I do not feel too out of the ordinary. For everyone else that I come across, it is an overwhelming and shocking occurrence to see someone of my height. Odell Beckham Jr., NFL wide receiver, once said that at times he felt like a zoo animal because of the way people looked at him. Even though I am not a celebrity, I sometimes feel the same because of how infatuated people are with my height. They automatically stare at me every time I walk by or walk into a room. Not only this, but they make all types of comments about me, good and bad, pretending as if I cannot hear them. Some people want to stop me for pictures or ask a variety of questions: How tall are you? Do you play basketball? Where do you play at? What size shoes do you wear?

I have learned to embrace the attention, and I try to be as kind as possible in these situations that occur every time I leave the house. Often, I do not mind the remarks and understand that the general public often does not come in contact with someone who is 7 feet tall. However, there are other times, such as major sporting events or concerts, where some comments can be a bit overwhelming. If I go to a game in Dallas, every five steps I take I would hear, "HEY, DIRK!" or "PORZINGIS!" or "Why aren't you out there on the court?" I do not typically adjust my normal routine because of this, but it can be frustrating when everyone thinks that they have the funniest joke about my height, as if I have never heard it before. I have heard it all.

There have been times when people have gotten upset because they could not see over me and have yelled or tried to push me out of the way. I try to find seats where I can be on the aisle, with no one sitting behind me so that I don't have to feel like I'm messing up someone else's view.

It is also hard for me to fit into a lot of cars, and I have had to spend a whole lot of money on clothes, trying to figure out what will fit me. Airplanes can be a nightmare with no leg room and very cramped quarters that result in miserable flights.

Regarding basketball, I have had to deal with the pressure of feeling like I always have to succeed, be on a top-level team, and have it all together, just so I would be able to answer people's questions accordingly. I had to overcome the stereotypes of people thinking that my height was going to make me uncoordinated or not athletic. I have always felt like I needed to prove myself to the world whenever I step on the court. I've always been the target of people's attention, good or bad, and I have to maintain a sense of self-control to deal with all that is thrown at me.

College Basketball: A Player's Perspective

People tell me that I only got as far as I did because of my height and that if they were my size, they would have gotten so much farther. I think envy and jealousy also have something to do with this—at the end of the day, a lot of people would like to be tall. Shorter guys typically have something to say and prove, trying to maintain their masculinity by acting out and being crazy. Heavier guys think they can bully me around, assuming I am too weak for them.

Because of my height, I thought basketball was the only route for me, and if I did not make it to the NBA that I had failed. It has at times made me insecure, thinking that people only care for me on the surface but never want to actually get to know me or understand who I really am as a person.

Do I like being tall? All in all, I really do. The positives outweigh the negatives, and even though some might consider it a blessing and a curse, I am happy to deal with whatever comes my way. God has given countless memories and experiences that would not have happened if I did not stand out in the crowd, and I am thankful for every one of them. I know that the Lord made me tall for a reason, and I am comfortable in my own skin, and I don't want to change a thing about how He made me.

On December 1, 2018, I received a prophetic word from God through an elderly lady at a church in Scottsdale, Arizona. She said God had been speaking to her to ask me, *"Do you know why God made you tall?"* I replied, *"Umm, well, I'm not exactly sure."* She went on to say God had been telling her to tell me *"to be a leader and to seek Him."*

My Dream

My goal has been to seek God in all I do and use what he has blessed me with to lead people in the right direction and have a positive impact on everyone that I come across. I try to live by God's commandments, which include loving others and seeing them through God's eyes, remembering that we are all made in His image.

2

My Growing Up Years

My story begins on September 13, 1993, in Fort Worth, Texas. I consider myself fortunate to have been born into a Christian family. All I have ever known is a life that included God, the Bible, and prayer as an integral part of my every day. Therefore, I have had a firm foundation to stand on. Life is not always an easy road, so when the going gets tough, it is awesome to know you are not walking alone.

My parents were in their thirties and had been married for nine years when I was born. I have one sister, who is four years older than me. Unfortunately, my dad made the decision to leave my mom, my sister, and me when I was one year old. Obviously, I was not totally aware of the ramifications of his decision. When I was growing up, I had one parent, my mom. I have never experienced what it was like to have a dad around on a regular basis.

Knowing that God's design is for children to have two parents, I'm sure it was a disadvantage for me to grow up without a dad, but I didn't know any different. That was a normal life for me. And I firmly believe that God has been with me every step of the way, filling any void, being a perfect Father to me.

Thankfully, my mom and I have always been close. She has always been my biggest fan, encourager, and supporter. My mom was always there to make sure my needs were met, help with school projects, drive me to practices and games, cheer me on in the stands (she never missed a game), listen whenever I needed to talk, take care of me when I was sick, cook for us, and just be consistently present and available.

    My mom was a school teacher. She taught in the Christian school I attended. We never had much money, no extra money to go on vacations, but she provided a lot for us, and I never felt like I lacked for anything. My mom, my sister, and I rode to school together every day.

    I have also been fortunate to be blessed with loving grandparents on my mom's side. I have many fond memories of fun times with them over the years.

Easter, Age 3.

First day of kindergarten, Age 6.

Getting the latest copy of Sports Illustrated for Kids. I was always excited and read it cover to cover.

My grandparents,
Joe and Marilyn Breshears,
who mean the world to me.

College Basketball: A Player's Perspective

They have prayed for me daily and have been a constant encouragement and support.

I have always loved sports, and so much of my life has revolved around them. Even the video games I played in my younger years were all sports related.

I played baseball and basketball. During my younger years, baseball was my main sport. I was selected as an all-star every year I played. As I got older, I decided to concentrate on basketball.

Every school year, I was consistently a head taller than any of my classmates. From the day I was born, I had always been off the growth charts (over 100%) in height, year after year.

My growth was steady, and there were no big growth spurts, but I continued to grow taller until I peaked at 6 feet 11 1/2 inches (7 feet with my shoes on) in high school. I have always had the reputation of being nothing but kind to my classmates and friends. Unfortunately, some years, I did not have the nicest teachers, and I never really enjoyed school to begin with. But I tried to do my best as a student, knowing that was the right thing to do. I attended one Christian school for kindergarten and first grade. Then, my mom, sister, and I transferred to another Christian school for Grades 2 through 6. This is where I first played basketball for my school and had a positive winning experience.

I have always had a passion for sneakers.

Fun times playing for my grandpa, Age 5.

I spent many hours playing basketball inside, when I needed a break from the outdoors.

My all-star team, Age 5.

My Growing Up Years

We changed schools again for seventh grade. The transition that year was tough. The coach at that time hardly played me at all in games for at least half of the season. This was upsetting to me. I almost quit the team and even contemplated giving up basketball. The coach finally gave me a chance to play in a tournament game; I scored a lot of points in that game, so he then realized I could play and gave me more minutes from then on. My final year of middle school was much better; however, I was still not considered to be one of the top players.

During this transition from middle school to high school, I was blessed with a really cool experience. I was given the opportunity to go on a two-game road trip with the Dallas Mavericks. I flew on the team's plane, stayed in the same hotel with the team, rode on the bus with them to the arena, went in the entrance they walked in, watched their warm-ups courtside, and even got to guard one of the players during warm-ups. I got to have my picture taken with several of the Mavericks. I met Mark Cuban, owner of the Mavericks, and he promised to "save a spot for me on the team."

That trip was memorable and motivated me to continue pursuing my dream. I remember not being ready to go home and have my time with the Mavericks end. I remember thinking I would love to live that lifestyle.

With Mark Cuban, owner of the Dallas Mavericks, and my father, Phil Rykhoek.

With Dirk Nowitzki, the legend.

In my freshman year of high school, the varsity coach wanted me on his team badly. Initially, I didn't want to move up to that team at all because I wanted to play with my peers; however, I ended up deciding to give the varsity team a chance. About halfway through that season, I became a starter and had a highly productive freshman year. I later realized how much this early transition helped me throughout the rest of my high school career, and I am thankful that I got this rare opportunity as a fifteen-year-old.

During the summer between my freshman and sophomore years, I dunked the ball for the first time. I continued to work on my jumping ability, so I was ready to make a big impression in year 2. As a sophomore, I made steady and consistent progress in becoming a better player. I became more comfortable playing with some of my classmates, and it showed in my performance. It wasn't until one of our biggest games of the season, though, that I took my game to the next level.

We were playing our archrival school, and I dunked on someone in front of a packed crowd. The place went crazy, and I was feeling great. The highlight was later broadcasted on the local news and gave me my first taste of how good I could be. This gave me confidence that carried on for the rest of the season. My stats continued to rise, and our team won more games.

The following summer, I decided it was time to play my first season of AAU (select) basketball. This was a big change and an eye-opening experience. At this level, not only is the competition higher, as the top players from their respective schools are now playing

College Basketball: A Player's Perspective

against each other, but the spotlight shines brighter as well. I did not fully understand what I was getting into, but I stumbled upon a familiar coach with a sponsored organization, so I decided to give it a shot.

    At age sixteen, I was a well-rounded and skilled basketball player after so many years of experience playing the game, but I was also very shy and sometimes lacked assertive-aggressive behavior. My game was based on skill as opposed to a rough, physical style of play. Even though I was pushing 7 feet tall, I was coordinated and athletic. I could bring the ball down the court and do things that were typically reserved for guards. I was ambidextrous in that I am right-handed, but I shoot and play basketball as much with the left hand as I do the right. When you join a new team, particularly as a big man, you tend to be put in a box and are unable to showcase all of your abilities. Unfortunately, this was the case for all of my basketball career.

    I showed up to the first practice for my new team and did not really know where I fit in. The players were the same age as me but had been playing in this environment for several years. Eventually, I became comfortable with the level of play and was able to settle down and just have fun as I had always done before. I bonded with my teammates, figured out that I was a key component of the team, and scored at a high level.

My new team and I traveled around the country, playing in some of the top tournaments. College coaches were present in the gyms and would occasionally stop by to watch our team play. Overall, AAU turned into a pleasant and enjoyable experience.

Unfortunately, the coach had something against me that to this day I still do not understand. He was constantly yelling at me to be more physical, dunk the ball, and did not appreciate anything I did.

I tried to not pay too much attention to all of this because I was still dominating as a player, just not in the way the coach wanted me to.

One day, after we had lost a big game, he pulled me to the side and told me that I was never going to be a division 1 player. This always stuck with me as some extra motivation because I knew that he was wrong and that I was going to make it to that level.

Shortly thereafter, maybe a month or so later, we played one of our last tournaments of the season, and I had a big game. My confidence did not waver despite this coach who consistently tried to bring me down, and I played harder than ever.

In the final game of the AAU season, I had a strong dunk, which was seen by a college coach watching close by. After he saw what had happened, he came over to watch the rest of the game, and at the end of the AAU season, I received my first division 1 scholarship offer. I was happy, but not totally satisfied with the offer because I knew I wanted to end up at a college that was in a major conference. Regardless, I was the first division 1 basketball recruit in my school's 50+ year history.

College Basketball: A Player's Perspective

My high school junior year season was relatively easy for me. The basketball experiences the previous summer had transformed me into a new player, and I had no problem navigating through my high school season. My performance was elevated personally, and our performance as a team started to improve as well. People took notice and recognized what we, a small Christian school, were doing.

Once my junior season was over, I had a big decision to make. The next summer was my second and last year to play AAU basketball, and I needed a new team. I had an offer to play with one of the most prestigious teams in the area that played at the top level, the Nike EYBL. This was tempting to me, but I felt more comfortable playing with familiar players and coaches from our school's district. We had just as talented a team, if not more so, and had one of the best lineups in the region. We played in some high-profile events and always put on a show. I stayed with this team, and looking back, I'm glad I took this route, as I've built some great relationships that I still maintain to this day.

Everything was really coming along, and my stock rose by the game. I was still relatively unknown by coaches and evaluators around the country, but that was all about to change. We always had a crowd at our games because we had some top-ranked players in the country. I started and played a significant role in our team's success. I did not try to do too much but instead did whatever I could to help our team win games. I knew I was not one of the stars on the team, but I also knew I had the talent to compete with anyone.

My first big break was when I got invited to the Pangos All-American Camp in California. This invitation was for roughly the top 150 players in the nation. I played well, had some interviews, and ended up making the top 40 all-star game at the end of the camp. This was huge for me, and I was a little shocked at how far I had come in such a short period of time.

However, as was the case for most of my career starting at this point, there tended to be something bad that happened along with the good. My backpack got stolen right before I was about to play in the all-star game. I had brand new headphones, a new cell phone, my wallet, and clothes inside, and it was all taken. I did not know how I was going to get back home to Texas. The camp director called everyone together to see if anyone had information. Fortunately, after the game was over, they found my wallet with my ID left in it. All the cash was gone, but at least I could catch my flight.

Later on that summer, one of my best accomplishments to date was realized. I was invited to the Nike Skills Academies, which at the time included the Amare Stoudemire Skills Academy for the big men, and the LeBron James Skills Academy following that, which included the top players from all positions. I started off at the Amare Stoudemire camp in Chicago, Illinois. This was a highly exclusive group of what was understood to be the top 20 big men in the country. Similarly, the LeBron camp was for the top 100 players overall.

At the Amare camp, I was overwhelmed, because I did not know a single person there. Most of the players had been there before or knew other top-

College Basketball: A Player's Perspective

ranked players from previous events. I had no one to relate to and was having a tough time. When we would play 5v5 or normal game situations, I did well and showed my skills, but when we went into drills, I did not know what I was doing. I had not had much skill coaching up to this point, as my previous coaches typically just let me play however I wanted to. The footwork and other technical skills these players knew were beyond me. To this day, I never look overly impressive in drills due to the poor coaching I received throughout my life, but when it comes to scrimmaging, I can play with anyone. I spent most of my time growing up playing pickup games to develop my craft. Back to the Amare camp, I was slowly but surely starting to gain momentum and play well in front of the NBA scouts in attendance, when it all went wrong once again. I was playing in a combined game with the Deron Williams Skills Academy. Amare Stoudemire and Deron Williams were officiating the game. Suddenly, I got elbowed in the eye and almost instantly blacked out. I could not see, and a cut right above my eye was bleeding heavily. I was soon transported to the emergency room with my eye totally swollen shut. The cut above my eye required multiple stitches, and I had to wear an eye patch for the next several days. I could not see out of my left eye for a couple of days, and because of the injury to my eye, I had to leave Chicago and go back home. Not only did I miss the rest of the camp, but I also didn't receive the photo that I had taken with Amare at the beginning of the skills academy. This was disappointing because I have always enjoyed meeting and having a photo opportunity with people at the top of their profession.

After I had been home a while, unable to work out, I became out of shape. I was a little scarred from all that had transpired and did not know what to do. The LeBron James Skills Academy was on the calendar for the following week, and I was not ready physically or emotionally. I declined to go to the camp, which later turned out to be a big regret. Even though I was unable to participate due to the eye injury, they offered me the opportunity to still attend the camp, pick up valuable gear that each participant received, meet LeBron James, and have my photo taken with him. I decided I did not want to go. I was unsure of myself at the time, and looking back, I know that not attending the LeBron camp was a mistake.

Instead of going to the camp, I decided to play with my AAU team that weekend. At that point in the summer, I was nationally ranked right after the top 100 players, around number 20 for my position. College coaches were calling me nonstop, and I was picking up scholarship offers by the day. Finally, people were starting to think highly of my game, and I could have gone to almost any school in the country, except for the upper-echelon group of Duke, Kansas, Kentucky, etc. Those schools were never an option for me. I know I would have been good enough, but I was a little late to the party, only playing AAU for a couple of years. When I came back from the eye injury, I was a little skittish. I did not want to get hit in the face again and suffer more problems there, so initially, I did not play as I had before. The summer ended, and my ranking dropped slightly.

First season of AAU basketball with Team Texas.

District battle against Isaiah Austin and Grace Prep.

Pangos Top 40 All-Star Game—Long Beach, CA.

Nike Skills Academy Chicago, IL.

During my senior year of high school, I felt unstoppable. I was averaging over 30 points per game and felt like I could make any play at any time on the court. I had a couple of game-winning buckets, one of which was in a tournament where I made an and-one free throw to win the game. In that same tournament, I broke the school record, scoring 40 points in a game. I broke that record again scoring 42 points the next day, combined with the previously mentioned game-winner.

When we would go on the road to play away games, I was heckled by the crowds heavily. In one game, we played a public school close to our private school, and they had a whole student section ready to yell at me when we walked in the gym close to an hour before game time. There was another game against a district opponent where they had my mom's picture on a cardboard cutout, with their school's logo on a bag she was holding in the picture. They screamed at me through a hole they cut in the middle of my mom's mouth on the picture.

It was very strange, but people went to great lengths to try and distract my team and me.

Going into Christmas, I was a "player to watch" in the highly acclaimed Whataburger Tournament. A few days prior to the tournament, I played in a pickup game without warming up properly and suffered an injury that ended up diminishing the entire rest of my playing career. I hurt my groin and could barely walk up the stairs. The local doctors thought it was only a strain, but it turned out to be much worse. This will all be explained later in the book.

College Basketball: A Player's Perspective

I finished the rest of my senior season, playing on and off sparingly, but it was a disappointing finish. However, I still ended the season averaging about 25 points and 10 rebounds a game. Our team won a playoff game but lost in the next round. Keep in mind, my groin remained an issue leading up to my arrival on a college campus.

One would think that throughout this highly accomplished high school career, I would have been loved and appreciated by my school, but for some reason, I was not. I did not do anything to deserve the treatment I received during these years, but a lot of people did not care for me. I was the first ever division 1 basketball recruit from the school, but the school staff acted like it was no big deal and initially did not want to allow me to have any type of signing day announcement. One reason for all this seemed to be due to religious ties since I did not go to the same church affiliate that the majority of the school went to. Another part was that the school seemed to not want to promote any sport other than football. In addition, I've since learned that there was a lot of jealousy over the attention I was receiving.

But for whatever reasons, to this day, I still feel like I am not even welcome back at my alma mater. It does not make much sense. A few years ago, when I went back to my high school, I received many negative comments from people asking why I had come back to visit. This made me a little bit sad because I feel like I did a lot for the school in regard to its basketball credibility.

I tried my best to be positive about that situation and continue being supportive of the players and coaches. I tried to encourage and help others, yet some treated me as if I am an enemy, even though I did not do anything bad to anyone. This just shows, no matter what you do, some people are going to have problems with you. They will make up lies and try to give you a bad name simply because they are insecure themselves and feel threatened by you, especially if you are more successful than they are. If you are better liked than they are, they cannot handle it and will do whatever it takes to try and bring you down. But, at the end of the day, even though I am not really able to show love to the school anymore, I am choosing to forgive all the wrong ways they have treated me and move on, being the bigger person in the situation. People may talk badly about me behind my back and lie about my character, but I do not want to engage with them anymore. All I know is that God truly knows the person that I am, and that is all that really matters. My reputation and whatever false rumors others might have heard about me do not define who I am. I can stand strong knowing that eventually the truth will be brought to light.

My mom holding a cardboard cutout of herself made by the opposing team to distract me in one of our games.

Grandpa Joe giving helpful advice and post game encouragement.

3

The College Recruiting Process

By the end of my senior year in high school, I had received countless division 1 offers to play basketball at the highest college level, my dream come true. It was an exciting time. College coaches were coming to watch me play. They were calling, emailing, and texting me. I saved a large container full of mail from colleges that were interested in recruiting me. The recruiting process was overwhelming at times. Very aware of how important the decision is, you definitely want to make the right choice, all the while feeling bombarded from all sides. It can be confusing to process all the information and try to visualize yourself at each school. The coaches make everything look and seem absolutely amazing, and they are very persuasive as they try to convince you how wonderful your experience would be if you were a part of their program.

My mom and I visited seven of the colleges. The visits were exhausting, full days of touring the campus and basketball facilities, talking to coaches, meeting faculty and players, discussing the academic part of the package, checking out the housing situation, getting a feel for the city, and trying to get an overall sense of whether or not that basketball program would be a good fit for me.

College Basketball: A Player's Perspective

I decided to sign with a Texas school relatively close to home. The deciding factor was the Christian element at this school; the coaches said they all love Jesus, they had Bible studies and prayed with the players, and there were Scriptures on the walls in the locker room. Given my Christian school background, along with the way I was raised, that seemed like the best fit for me.

What we later learned is that the recruiting process is not necessarily a clear picture of what it is actually like once you are on the inside and living the experience on a daily basis. The coaches will say whatever they need to say in the recruiting pitch to get you on board, but once you are, it is an entirely different "ball game." There is no more impressing.

They already have you, and you are now at the mercy of the coaching staff and their style and philosophy of coaching. Unfortunately, no coach figured out who I was as a person nor what coaching techniques would work to bring out the best in me.

After making the big decision regarding what university to choose, I moved to campus with nothing but high expectations (and naturally, some anxiety) in June of 2012, just days after my high school graduation. I was certain this was going to be a positive experience for me.

With my mom at college signing day at my high school.

First time with a college uniform on.

College Basketball: A Player's Perspective

In order to begin my college basketball workouts, I would attend both summer sessions. Daily workouts typically included early morning weights (before classes) and then cardio, extra lift, basketball practice, and open gym between 3 and 6 p.m., with an additional pool, boxing, or other workout thrown in randomly.

4

The Division 1 Basketball Experience: Freshman Year

Unfortunately, my expectations did not become a reality. The academic aspect was challenging but fine; the basketball experience was disappointing, and that is putting it mildly. My first day on campus was "a series of unfortunate events," and to my dismay, that pattern continued to play out.

Given that I had not received adequate strength and conditioning training during high school, my body was not ready for the extreme physical demands at the division 1 level. Initially, training was brutal for me. The workouts pushed me to the brink of throwing up and left my legs feeling like rubber. I was gassed. With time, the conditioning became easier as my body adapted and got in better shape.

During practices, I mainly guarded a teammate who was built for football and 280 pounds; he actually did go on to play in the NFL after college. I was 4-5 inches taller and weighed 50-60 pounds less. It was a daily battle. After practice, I was the one teammate left to get beat up on, helping others out with their "finishing drills" around the basket. Taking a lot of contact would be an understatement. I always ended up with bruises, sometimes jammed fingers, or a hyperextended arm. I felt like nothing more than a practice dummy.

College Basketball: A Player's Perspective

Early on, I got the impression that the coaches did not respect me, nor did they consider me a great player. Even though I was just as effective the majority of the time, I did not have the same hype and ranking behind me. I would later realize that a lot of NBA players take their high school success and status, go to college for a year, and use the name they have made for themselves to take them all the way to the NBA Draft. Even if they have a mediocre college season, teams will still take a chance on them. Given that this was the case, certain players are put on a pedestal and treated as if they are the whole team in its entirety. They garner all the attention and publicity, and the coaches feed off of it. The coaches want them to fulfill all these expectations, so they give them no sort of repercussions. They get away with whatever they want and are allowed unlimited mistakes. I knew I just needed some time to work myself up to that level later in my career.

Early on, the coaches worked with me to change my shot, which messed me up and affected my confidence. The coaches' philosophy was to tear down the athlete, I guess in an attempt to motivate them. But that approach did not motivate me.

The last thing I wanted was to be redshirted. In fact, had I known that would happen, I would not have gone to that school. Regardless, the coaching staff decided to redshirt me my freshman year so I could gain weight and experience since our frontcourt was stacked.

Even though we already had an abundance of height and talent, all the players on the team wanted me to play and knew I could contribute to the team's success. My teammates petitioned all year long for the coaches to take away my redshirt label since I consistently had great practices.

If one of our players had gotten dismissed from the team prior to the season, I would have gotten to play, and who knows how differently things would have turned out. The coaching staff continued to consider taking away my redshirt at different points, but as it turned out, the only games I got to play in my first year of college were our exhibition game and a couple of scrimmages.

I contemplated quitting more than once, but I knew I could not. There were days when I felt like I was physically, mentally, and emotionally done. At some points, I felt like I hated everything about basketball. I thought that it was all political, and I felt like I was constantly fighting an uphill battle. I had to combat feeling discouraged and overcome thoughts that I couldn't do this anymore. I recall wishing I could fast forward four years.

During a December workout, I hurt my groin again. This had happened one other time during my senior year of high school. I made the coaches and trainer aware of the injury, but I was told to continue practicing, so I did. I continued to practice for another four months, which caused the problem to become chronic. Months later, the opposite groin began to feel the same way.

Both sides were now badly injured! The trainer attempted to treat the groin with hot/cold tub, pre-practice bicycle warm-ups, steroid injections, etc. But the coaches thought I was faking it or trying to get out of things, so I was expected to practice with two injured groins until basketball season ended. As it turned out, the season lasted longer than any other previous season, because we went all the way to the NIT Championship in April and won the title. I was hurting big time!

5

Surgery Number One: Postseason and Summer after Freshman Year

Much to my dismay, I had the shingles at the end of my freshman year of college—my body's reaction to the stress of the year. My doctor said the steroid injections I received to relieve the groin pain probably weakened my immune system, which led to shingles.

I scheduled a variety of treatments in an attempt to help the groin issue. The therapist who helped me with my treatments researched the symptoms I described to her and came to the conclusion that I might have a hernia. On her recommendation, I went to see a doctor in Denton, Texas, and was diagnosed with an inguinal hernia. It was a relief to find out what I thought was causing the groin pain I had been enduring for months during basketball practices.

To repair the hernia, I had surgery on June 28, 2013. The recovery for this surgery was a few months. I was hopeful this would be the remedy for the groin pain. To my dismay, after recovering from the hernia surgery, the groin pain continued when I played basketball.

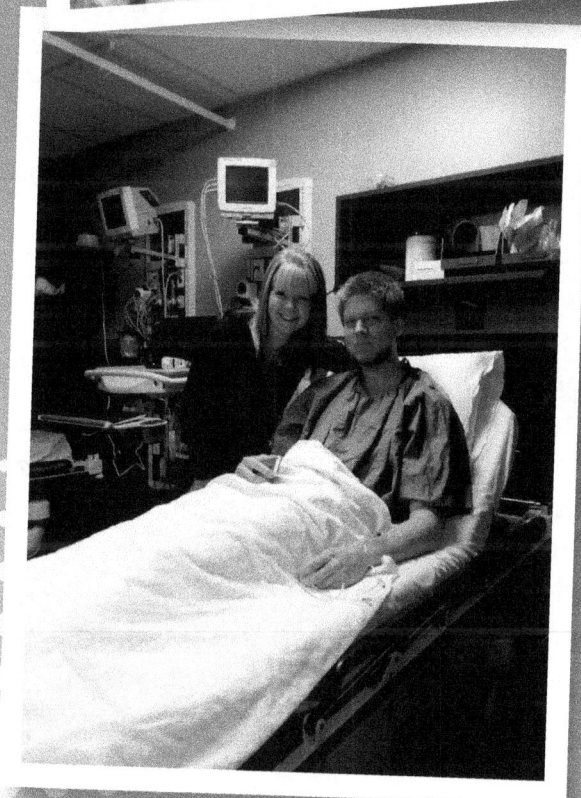

6

Surgery Number Two: End of First Semester of Sophomore Year

The university flew me to Nashville to be seen by a doctor who specialized in sports medicine. The doctor concluded that I needed to have surgery on my right hip to correct impingement. I had excess bone buildup on my hip joint that caused the impingement, which in turn, led to a labrum tear. My right hip surgery to repair the torn labrum and shave off excess bone buildup was performed in Nashville on December 27, 2013. Months of physical therapy and rehab followed.

Due to the injury and surgery, I was now considered medically exempt for my sophomore year. The rehab process was long and slow. I had to be on crutches for a month and could not drive, which made it difficult to get to classes, the gym, and physical therapy. My mom had to camp out at college with me for that month to help and drive me around. After a month, I could gradually put weight on my right foot and leg and continue the PT protocol for additional months. Then, I had to put in the work to get my strength and conditioning back to game-ready status.

I thought for sure the right hip surgery would be the fix, and the groin pain would subside. But again, that was not the case. Even after I recovered from the right hip surgery, I continued to have groin pain when I played basketball.

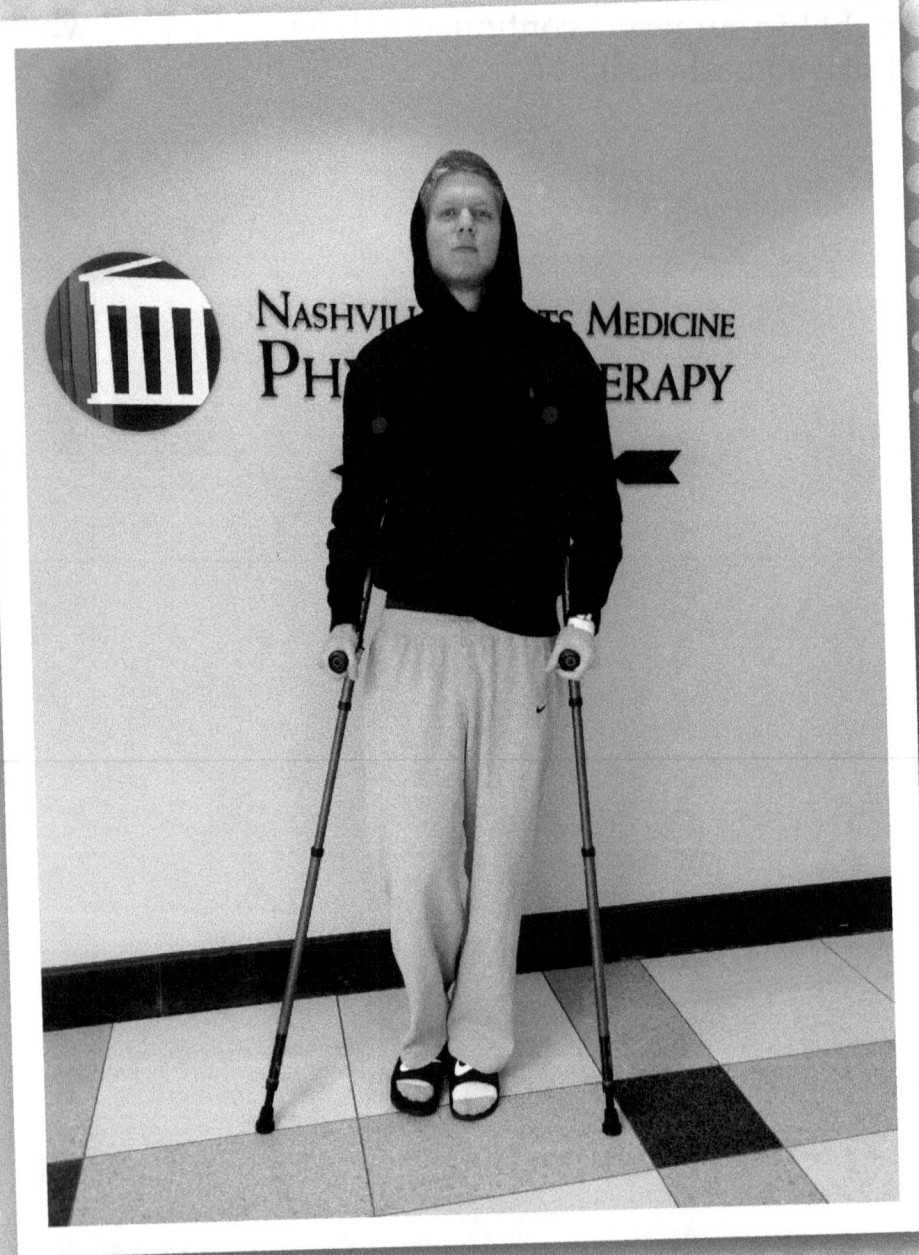

7

Surgery Number Three: Second Semester of Sophomore Year

The next step was to see a doctor in Philadelphia who is well-known for his work with core-related injuries. MRIs revealed that my groin was "shredded" on both sides. So, I was scheduled for double groin surgery on March 27, 2014. Once again, after surgery, I worked through a physical therapy regiment for the remainder of the year while having to regain strength and conditioning. Surely, repairing the shredded groin muscles would be the cure. I thought now I would finally be able to play basketball free of pain. But, unfortunately, even after double groin surgery, I continued to experience groin pain.

I returned to the institute in Philadelphia where I was advised that I needed left hip surgery given that my left hip had the same impingement the right hip had because of excess bone buildup. The left labrum was torn as well and in need of repair.

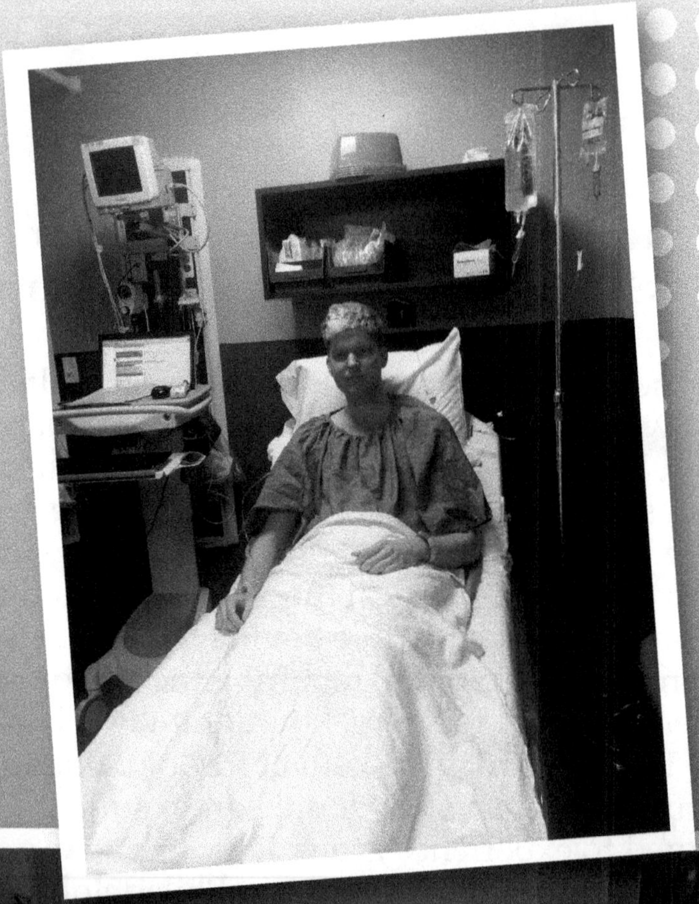

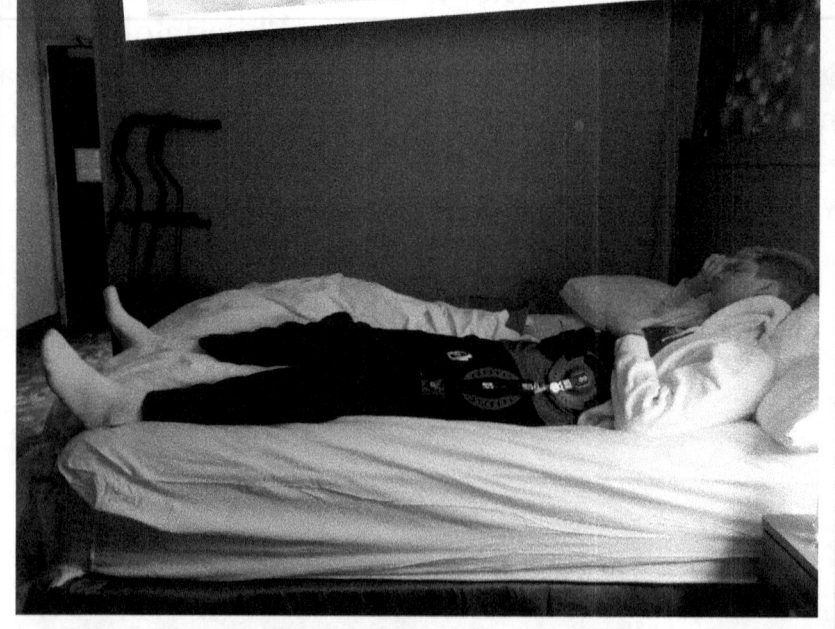

8

Surgery Number Four, Five, Six, and More

Surgery number four on the left hip was scheduled for March 5, 2015, in Philadelphia. And once again, I did physical therapy for months afterward, followed by rehab. In addition to the multiple core-related surgeries, due to the stress of all that I had endured and subsequent clenching and grinding, I developed TMJ (ear fullness, limited jaw mobility, chronic jaw aching/pain) and had to end up having two TMJ-related surgeries. Neither surgery relieved the TMJ symptoms, so I continue to deal with jaw and ear discomfort and keep trying to seek a remedy or solution that would give me relief for the first time in five-plus years. I also developed kidney stones during my last semester of college and had to drive myself to the local emergency room in excruciating pain. To this day, I am so weary of medical issues, doctor visits, procedures, and recoveries.

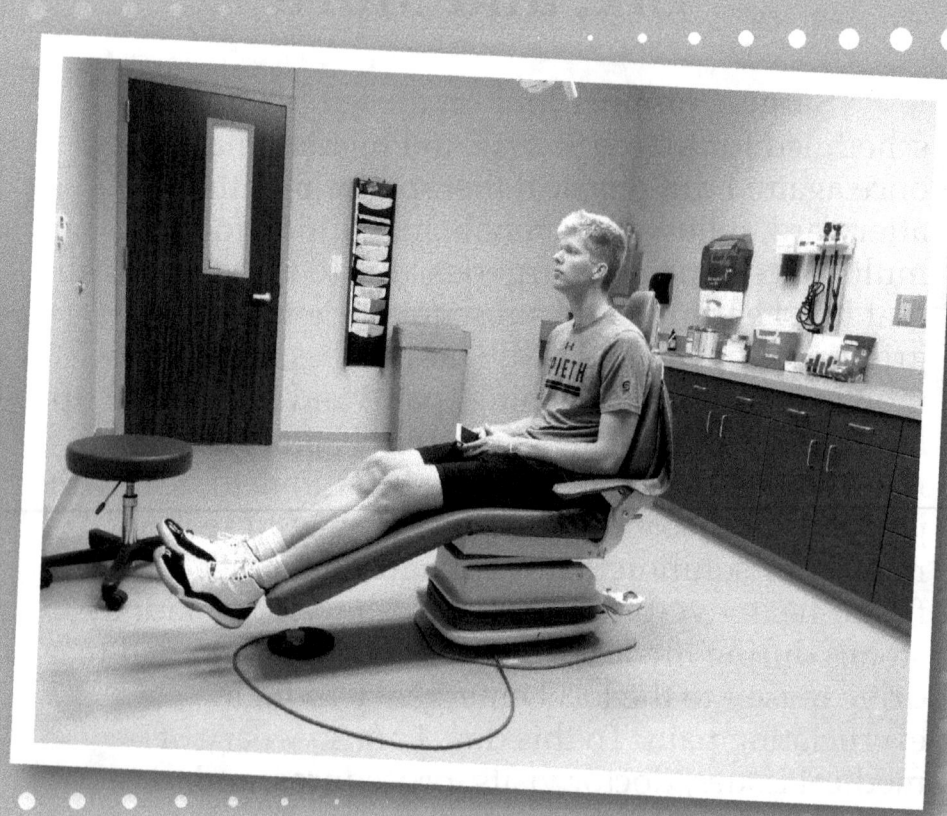

9

From Medical Exempt to Medical Release

It was now clear that I was not going to be able to participate at the high level of basketball play the university needed from me, so my status changed from medical exempt to medical release, and I was no longer on the basketball team. The day I had to sign the paperwork was an extremely hard day. I had been playing on a basketball team for most of my life. Now, due to injuries and multiple surgeries over the course of two years, being a part of a team came to a screeching halt.

During my junior and senior years of college, I would simply be a college student, no longer a student-athlete. The university was generous to continue paying for my tuition and room and board, as well as all of my medical bills. What an incredible blessing it was to have all of my college expenses paid for, as well as the cost of multiple surgeries.

10

The Transition from Student-Athlete to Student and College Graduation

    Initially, I struggled to find my identity and purpose during this transitional period from student-athlete to student only. I had never been one who liked school, but I had been passionate about sports my entire life. I lived to compete, especially at the game of basketball. So, what now? I focused on finishing my undergraduate course work. It was an extremely tough task to obtain a business degree from this university.

    My last year and a half, I felt like I was constantly working on a school project or scheduled to be at a group meeting. I am not sure how I would have completed these full-time course loads had I still been on the team. This became another blessing in disguise because I was able to get my degree while maintaining a good GPA.

    In addition to these rigorous classes, I was commuting back home, driving an hour and a half each way, multiple times a week, to go to physical therapy. As much as I wanted to do well in school, I also wanted to get back on the basketball court. I wore myself out, took full loads during summer school, and did whatever it took to graduate as soon as possible. I had one goal in mind, and that was to be completely

The Transition from Student-Athlete to Student and College Graduation

healthy so that when I got my diploma, I was ready to hoop again.

By the time I graduated from college, I was beaten down. I had been treated in such a way that left me feeling disrespected, not valued, and less than confident. I don't think the coaching staff ever appreciated the kind of young man I am, nor do I think they ever believed I was a great basketball player. I would later leave this institution and athletic program with negative feelings regarding my basketball experience. My only positive takeaways were some memorable moments.

However, I had great teammates who have all gone on to be professional athletes and do big things, and I am very grateful I got the chance to be their teammate and watch their success unfold.

The best physical therapists—Dale Smith and Lyndsy Bedell (not pictured, Mike McQuaid).

Cory Jefferson, played for Brooklyn Nets/Phoenix Suns; Allerik Freeman, professional basketball; John Heard, successful businessman; Isaiah Austin, professional basketball; Kenny Chery, professional basketball; Ishmail Wainwright, 2-sport professional athlete; Gary Franklin, successful entrepreneur; Royce O'Neale, Utah Jazz; Taurean Prince, Atlanta Hawks; Johnathan Motley, Dallas Mavericks/LA Clippers (Not pictured, Rico Gathers, Dallas Cowboys).

Cory Jefferson played for Brooklyn Nets and Phoenix Suns.

Pierre Jackson, drafted by Philadelphia 76ers, played for Dallas Mavericks.

John Heard and Logan Lowery, real-world professionals.

Johnathan Motley, NBA; Josh Clemons, veteran and successful in business.

Emmanuel Mudiay, AAU teammate and high school district opponent, drafted by Denver Nuggets, plays for the New York Knicks at Madison Square Garden.

I really love to support and encourage my former teammates in their journey, because they were always so supportive of me during my time in college. Each teammate brought something different to the table, and I have no issues whatsoever with any of them. I was fortunate to have so many terrific teammates.

But I was definitely ready to leave this school and have a fresh start. Thankfully, I was able to complete my undergraduate degree in business management in three and a half years, despite the multiple surgeries and recovery periods. I graduated a semester early in December 2015. This allowed me the chance to transfer without having to sit out an entire season. Since I had yet to play in any real games in my career, I didn't want to sit out any longer, and this was my best chance to succeed in the short term, by graduating as quickly as possible.

11

What Now? What Next?

I always knew I would return to playing basketball. I was determined to. There was no way I was going to go through all of the heartache, spend all these years training, and not accomplish this goal. I spent the spring semester of 2016 at home, working out to get back in shape. I worked out on my own for the most part. I was never too fond of trainers or working with them, but I did at times, and I also had some good friends who helped me out.

I believe the more you play the game of basketball, running up and down the court, 5v5, the better player you will be. I focused on playing, as well as lifting weights, to maintain a certain level of strength. One recommendation I have for young athletes would be to stay away from trainers who are only out to get your money and neglect giving assistance with techniques that would benefit you in real game situations. I know players who perform well during drills, but do not know how to play well in a real game.

12

Moving on for a Master's Degree

I decided to go to another university to begin work on my master's degree and play basketball. This was a lot different than years past because instead of all the coaches reaching out to recruit me, I had to reach out to them via email and try to convince them I could still play. Also, my previous school banned me from transferring to another university in the same conference.

After putting the word out regarding my intentions, I only had a handful of high-level division 1 schools interested in giving me a basketball scholarship for graduate study. Already, the effect of past injuries was coming into play. Most people thought my career was over and that there was no way I could still be effective after all my body had been through.

Thankfully, God opened doors, and I had options to play at some big-name universities and programs. After much thought and prayer, I narrowed my choices. It came down to a decision between two schools. After visiting both, I felt led to go to a university in Tennessee.

Moving on for a Master's Degree

Having learned some things during the first go-round of the recruiting process, I thought I would be able to discern even better this time around which school would be the best for me. Once again, I did my research and went with the school where I thought I could contribute the most and the one that seemed to be the best fit for me.

In August of 2016, I moved to Tennessee. This was going to be my big return to college basketball. The city's newspaper had several articles related to my comeback. I was excited and had worked hard to get back to playing. I knew I would have to prove myself since I am the tall white guy, but I was determined to do just that. **I would be the only NCAA player to have ever played at the graduate level having never played in a game at the undergraduate level.** I earned the respect of my new teammates soon after starting practice and anticipated a great basketball season. A perk to playing for this university was that we played our games in an NBA arena. All things considered, I expected it to be a breakthrough year and a splendid comeback for me.

Rykhoek could be 'big' help

Transfer doing 'whatever it took' to play this season

PHIL STUKENBORG
PHIL.STUKENBORG@COMMERCIALAPPEAL.COM

A late-week University of Memphis basketball practice has ended at the Finch Center and Chad Rykhoek, who has a media interview request, walks briskly off the court and into the practice center's lobby. A folding chair awaits, although it hardly seems capable of comfortably accommodating his 6-foot-11 frame.

If the seating is less than ideal, Rykhoek isn't complaining. If the post-practice obligation is delaying his departure, he isn't showing any disdain. Why should he?

See **RYKHOEK**, Page 7D

University of Memphis big man Chad Rykhoek runs through a drill with the team during their first practice Wednesday.

NIKKI BOERTMAN / THE COMMERCIAL APPEAL

However, right away, the coaches here tried to change my shot. Again. As a result, my confidence plummeted. During practices, I was the player who undeservedly received the most screaming and cursing from the coaches. I took the verbal lashings respectfully and did not yell or curse back, and despite all this, I consistently performed really well in practice.

When the season began, four of our starters were hometown players and played the entire game. I was the fifth starter, but when I was taken out of the game, I hardly got back in. I didn't get nearly as many minutes as I should have gotten. The players even complained to the coaches frequently about me not being in the game. And when I was in the game, I didn't get many touches, so my stats weren't great. I was told not to shoot during games. I was told to definitely not shoot 3-pointers even though that was something I'd been doing my whole life at a high percentage of accuracy. I did what I was told, but I felt like a robot and definitely did not feel free at all to play "my game."

This made it hard to fit in and find my role during the games. When you make one mistake and get pulled out of the game, it's hard to be confident and play like normal. Additionally, when the bright lights come on and the coach has no control over the team or the offense, there is not always a lot of ball movement.

I didn't get a chance to do much and felt like a fraction of the player that I could be. It was frustrating for sure to feel like I had so much more to contribute, but I was not given the opportunity to.

Friend, Luke Storey, watching my first college basketball game.

13

Another Disappointing Injury and Setback

My in-game performances had been getting better and better, and I was finally starting to get into a groove. I had several strong games and was becoming more consistent. My best game of the season was our first nationally televised game in a Florida tournament. I had the tendency to really focus and play my best when I knew there was a national audience watching. This was also our first game against a top-quality opponent. I got a lot of publicity and had a breakout game. Things were going great, I was scoring the ball steadily, and my teammates were looking for me.

Later in the second half, our coach decided to sub me out for rest, but then never put me back in the game. We lost the game and the coach was heavily questioned as to why I was on the bench. He realized he messed up but did pretty much the same thing the next game, and I hardly played.

Then we had a home game where I played against a couple of my former AAU teammates and friends. It was another solid performance for me. People from my hometown came to the game, and I felt great. I had one of my better games, and things were looking up.

Je'lon Hornbeak, AAU teammate, Pangos roommate, high school district opponent, professional basketball player.

On the program cover with Dedric Lawson, star at University of Kansas, soon to be professional basketball player.

Another Disappointing Injury and Setback

In December of 2016, our team played against the University of Oklahoma. A group of family and friends had traveled to Oklahoma from Fort Worth, Texas, to watch me play. I had looked forward to this game with great anticipation. It was relatively close to home. I knew I would have a fan base, and I was excited that this game would be televised on CBS.

Shortly before halftime, I jumped up to go get an offensive rebound. When my feet hit the floor, my left ankle dislocated and my foot went sideways. I was on the floor for a few minutes trying to be cool despite the intense pain I was experiencing. Honestly, seeing my foot like that freaked me out. The OU team and coaching staff displayed great sportsmanship by coming over to encourage me. My mom was called down to the floor. I was taken off the court on a stretcher, on national television. The arena gave me a nice ovation. The commentators were telling my story during the injury delay, commenting on how sad this was given how much I had already been through in the past. I had so hoped and prayed that I would have no more medical issues. This ankle dislocation was absolutely devastating!

After they took me off the court on a stretcher, I was taken to the training room. OU's team doctor was a well-known and respected orthopedic surgeon. He asked if there was any anesthetic available and was told no. He then proceeded to reset and splint my foot before I realized what he was actually doing. That was the most pain I had ever experienced, more pain than any of my previous surgeries. I let out a scream that was heard in the other room.

The doctor said it would take something "violent" for an ankle dislocation like that to occur. I tried to be strong despite my extreme disappointment. When they called my mom in the room to show us the X-rays, a few tears rolled down my cheeks. I thought that I would never get to play basketball again. I saw my whole career flashing before my eyes and felt like it was all over right then and there.

My friends who had come to watch me play joined us in the training room where we watched the rest of the game together. It was an encouragement to have all of them there.

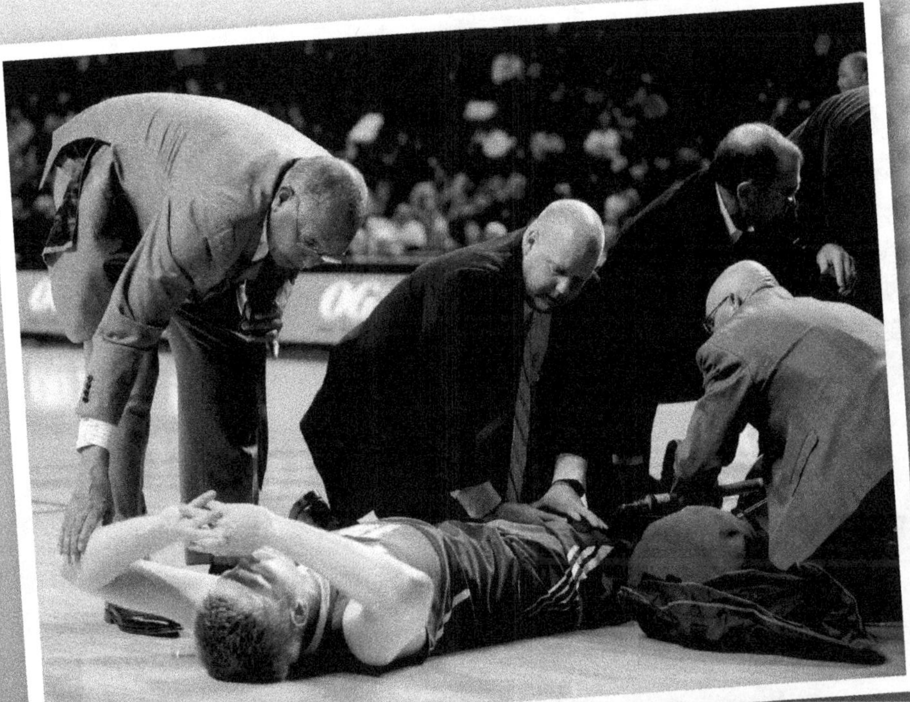

Much appreciation for the support I received from my teammates, Oklahoma players, coaches, and fans.

In the training room with friends from high school: Hayden Vinz, Parker Bow, Calle Reekie, and Damien Simpkins.

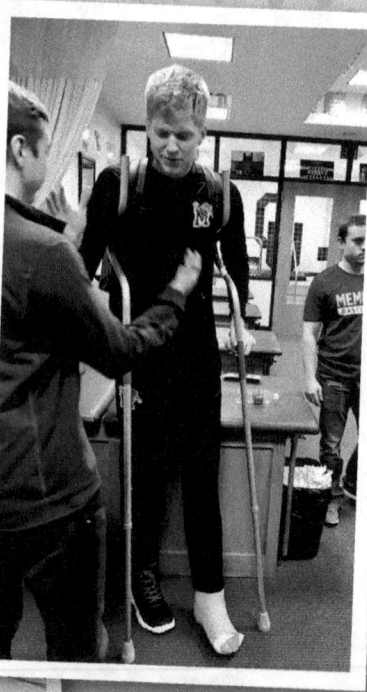

With teammate and friend from Dallas, Kaleb Castro.

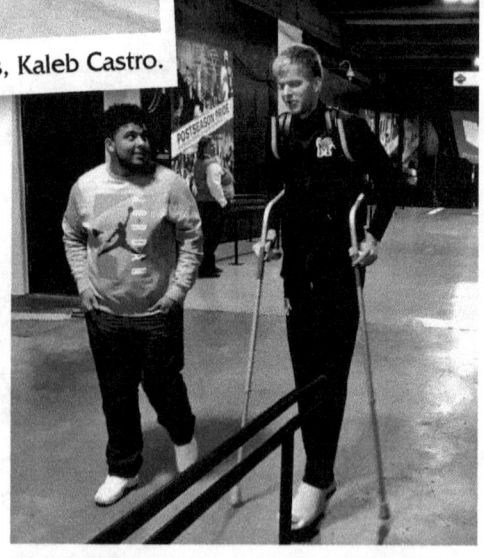

Another Disappointing Injury and Setback

The only positive from this experience was that I was trending on Twitter. I'm a big social media guy, so that was cool.

After the game, I boarded the team plane on crutches and headed back to Tennessee. X-rays taken after the swelling had gone down showed that there were no broken bones, so thankfully no surgery was needed at this time, just another long road to recovery, more physical therapy, and then another rehab to follow.

The doctor said I would be off the court for six to eight weeks. Given that time frame, I knew I could come back and play the last several games of the season. And I did just that. However, I really should not have been playing. The team was on a losing streak, and the basketball staff tried to rush me back on the court as soon as possible. They considered playing me in a big road game even though I had had very little practice but ended up seeing how the game went and waited a little longer.

Another Disappointing Injury and Setback

The first game of my return ended up being a huge conference road game on ESPN. During shootaround the day of, I could barely move. Both of my ankles felt terrible, since the other ankle had been overcompensating and was sprained. I thought there was no way that I should be on a court playing. But, as some of you may know, college basketball is a business, and I did not have a lot of say in the matter. I ended up playing a little bit in the game, not accomplishing a whole lot.

In the next game, I figured that I would be back in the regular rotation, since I had played in the game before and my foot was feeling slightly better. But much to my dismay, the coach put everyone in that game except for me, even the walk-ons! I felt incredibly disrespected and ended up voicing my opinion online, which resulted in an angry meeting with the coach.

Thankfully, we finally had our long-awaited game in my hometown of Dallas coming up. In the middle of warm-ups, one of the coaches informed me that I would once again be in the starting lineup. This brought me a lot of joy as it was another nationally televised game with a lot of famous people in the crowd, including former President George W. Bush and current Mavericks head coach Rick Carlisle. I even shared a greeting with George W. Bush during warm-ups, which is a moment I will never forget.

College Basketball: A Player's Perspective

I really appreciated the gesture to resume my starting position in this game, as I felt like I had worked back into playing shape and was able to contribute, despite my ankles being wrapped up so heavily that I could hardly move my feet. Unfortunately, our team got blown out. I did not touch the ball enough to even get a shot attempt up, and I was charged with several foul calls. My homecoming game was a disaster, and when I got subbed out for fouls, we were already losing so embarrassingly bad that I didn't even want to go back in the game.

In the last couple of games, including senior night, I still did not get a lot of playing time, but it felt good to be back on the basketball court again. What I failed to realize was that, all this time, my ankle was being severely damaged even more. This led to another surgery and over a yearlong recovery process that I will further describe later.

Unfortunately, our team did not perform well at the end of the season and missed the postseason. However, this was really another blessing because I was not in any condition to continue playing basketball with two bad ankles. But the town's newspaper articles about me were encouraging: Rykhoek keeps coming back.

With Christian Kessee, fellow graduate transfer, and Markel Crawford, current professional basketball player.

SPORTS

THE COMMERCIAL APPEAL • THURSDAY, FEBRUARY 16, 2017 COMMERCIALAPPEAL.COM/SPORTS

U OF M BASKETBALL

Memphis forward Rykhoek keeps coming back to play

MARK GIANNOTTO
USA TODAY NETWORK – TENNESSEE

Initially, a mass of people stood up behind the Memphis bench and blocked Teri Crisco's view. She couldn't see what happened almost two months ago at Oklahoma's Lloyd Noble Center. Just the aftermath, with her son laying there on the court, his hands interlocked behind his head.

She knew that meant Tigers forward Chad Rykhoek was in pain, and so she began to cry.

Before long, Crisco had been escorted onto the floor. She wiped away the tears, determined to show strength in the wake of another setback. She told Rykhoek this was all simply part of God's plans and he nodded his head ever so slightly.

"What else can you say when you're looking at his foot and it's going sideways?" Crisco said Wednesday.

Crisco will again be in the crowd Thursday night when Memphis travels to Connecticut, not wanting to miss Rykhoek's potential return to action from a gruesome dislocated ankle suffered on Dec. 17. He took part in his first full practice on Tuesday and Coach Tubby Smith indicated the 6-foot-11 Fort Worth, Texas, native could play after missing the past 15 games.

Whenever Rykhoek comes back, though, it will add to a story that is as remarkable as it is resilient.

A former top 150 recruit in 2012, Rykhoek arrived at Memphis last August, just shy of his 23rd birthday, to college basketball's first graduate transfer to have never appeared in a college game. What began as a tweaked groin during his senior year of high school turned into five surgeries and endless hours of rehabilitation at Baylor.

See RYKHOEK, Page 4C

Tigers' next game

Who: Memphis (18-8, 8-5) at Connecticut (12-12, 7-5)
When, where: 8 p.m. today, XL Center
TV, radio: ESPN2; WREC-AM 600, WEGR-FM 102.7

MARK WEBER/THE COMMERCIAL APPEAL
University of Memphis forward Chad Rykhoek (left) dunks in front of Jackson State defenders Demetrice Clopton (middle) and Maurice Rivers (right) in a game at FedExForum.

Another Disappointing Injury and Setback

By the time the season was over, I knew I could not return to this university and play under these coaches, given how this year had gone. I was the first player to let the coaches know I was transferring, only hours after the season had officially concluded. This started a trend and by the time it was over, only two scholarship players ended up staying for the next year. Three hometown guys who started each game and played the entire time every game opted to transfer as well. Another player's father said, "There is no way he would put his son through that 'torture' another year." It was one of the largest numbers of transfers from a team ever! Clearly, there was a problem. Looking back, all of us are now in a better place and glad we moved on.

My plan was to apply to the NCAA for a sixth year of eligibility, which I was certain I would be granted due to consecutive years of injuries and surgeries. But I would need to figure out where I should play for a sixth season.

With teammates Christian Kessee and Jeremiah Martin.

With teammates Christian Kessee and Markel Crawford.

14

Surgery Number Seven

After the season was over, the ankle I had dislocated at OU the past December continued to hurt when I played basketball. I was referred to a doctor in Southlake, Texas, who does stem cell injections to promote healing. After X-rays and 4 hours of MRIs on my feet and hips, the doctor determined I would benefit from a scope surgery to flush out debris that could have been what was causing the continued pain and discomfort in the dislocated foot. The doctor had envisioned that during the scope surgery, he would repair the internal damage caused by the dislocation and also inject stem cells harvested from my bone marrow and then mixed with amniotic tissue.

Surgery was scheduled for May 8, 2017. When the doctor started the process and looked inside my ankle, he realized it was a lot worse than it looked on the imaging. Clearly, my ankle was significantly more injured than previous doctors had led on, and there were a lot of problems that needed to be fixed. Once again, being forced to play on my ankle at the end of the season caused more damage to me in the long run. I had been having a hard time moving at all and for the right reason. There was a ligament tear in my ankle causing pain, as well as a plethora of debris resulting from my traumatic dislocation. Thankfully, I had found the right person for the job, and he got my ankle back to its intended state.

I ended up receiving six stem cell injections: three in the ankle I had dislocated, one in my right ankle that had been sprained several times, and one injection in both my left and right hips. The injections emit protein and other healing properties directly around the injured areas for up to six months.

Two months after the scope surgery and injections, I went in for a follow-up appointment with the doctor. He X-rayed my feet and hips and was both amazed and speechless at the results. My left foot that had suffered the dislocation injury did have a residual defect, but it was now on the road to being healed. The doctor was thrilled with the successful results of the stem cell injections. He said my feet and hips were going to be stronger than ever, so I was happy with the results.

However, I still had a lot of pain that had to be overcome. The recovery time was longer than any of my previous surgeries. My ankle was hurting for over a year before it started to feel better. This impacted my upcoming season and ended up forcing me to take even more time to be sure I was fully healed.

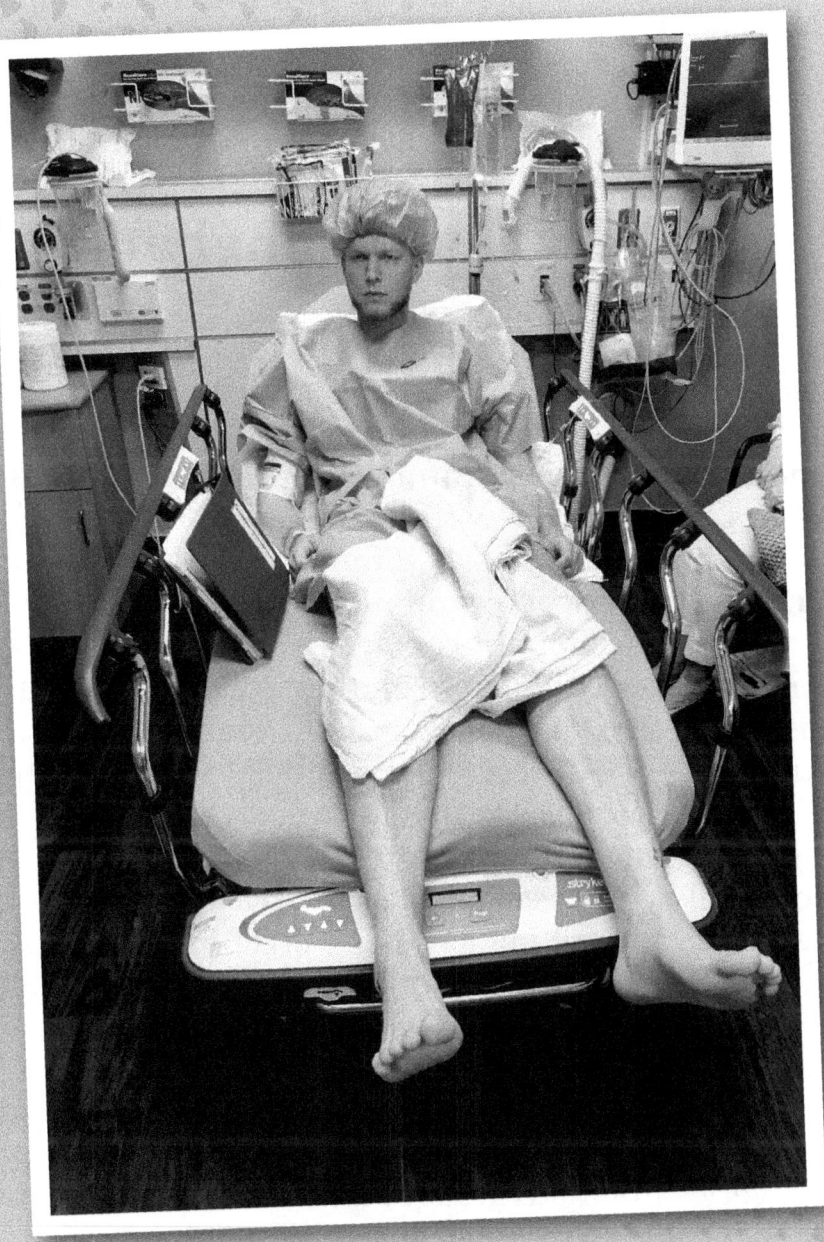

15

Back to Basketball for a Sixth-Year Comeback

Now, it was time to get the word out that I wanted to play one more year of college basketball. A number of schools contacted me. I visited at least six schools. Having been through the recruiting process twice, I thought I knew for sure what to look for. I did my research. It is important for me to like the conference, the school, and the coaching staff.

This selection process was especially important to me because I wanted to end my college career on a positive note with a successful full year of playing. On August 28, 2017, I received the official word that the NCAA had indeed granted me a sixth year of eligibility. But that decision came too late. It was technically past decision time. A division 1 school would have to submit another waiver to the NCAA and wait for that to be approved. I was very conflicted. My options were limited due to the last-minute eligibility approval.

Ideally, I wanted to go to division 1, but that did not seem feasible. The schools I had to choose from had very similar advantages and disadvantages. But when it came right down to it, I did not have 100% peace about going to either school. I made the difficult decision to end my college career and pursue a professional one, and at the same time continue to rehab and make sure my ankle was stable enough from the last surgery. I did not feel ready to play at a high level given the current pain in my feet and ankles. So, I chose to pursue other opportunities in the meantime.

16

The End of College Basketball in Pursuit of a Professional Career

So, what now?

What did God have in mind for me to do?

On August 12, 2017, at my home church, a woman spoke an encouraging prophetic word over me:

> "God has given you an inquisitive mind. You like to study things. You study people. You study life. You don't just take things at face value. The Lord likes that. Like the Bereans in Acts, they listened to the apostles' teaching and then compared to make sure what they heard lined up with the Word of God. There's a process coming in your life. God's going to allow you to understand some things as you seek, train, and study. Then, God is going to blow it all out of the water. You've gotten a little too safe.
>
> 'I'll do this if I can understand.'
>
> You are going to have enough knowledge to be able to discern what is of God and what is not of God. There are some things coming. He's going to mess with you a little bit.
>
> 'Now I want you to know Me in a way that you don't have to totally understand Me.'
>
> Trust. Be open. Don't shy away from it. To be forewarned is to be forearmed. Be ready. It's coming."

My job search began. *Colossians 3:23* reminds us, "Whatever you do, do it heartily as for the Lord, not for men."

The first job of interest I heard about was at a brand-new sports complex in the Dallas-Fort Worth metroplex. A former NBA player owns the facility. I applied, interviewed, and was hired to be one of the sports operations staff.

Around this same time, it seemed like God was also leading me to return to my high school alma mater to coach. The varsity boys' basketball coach had asked me to be an assistant under him. I wanted to give back. And I wanted to be the kind of coach I had always wanted, a players' coach. My goal was to treat the players with respect, value them as people, and be an encouragement to them. I ended up accepting the position as head coach for the freshman boys' team and as an assistant coach for the junior varsity and varsity teams.

My freshman team ended up with the best record. But, most importantly, I had good rapport with the players and received feedback from the parents that their sons enjoyed playing for me. Coaching for the first time was definitely a learning experience. I hope I made a positive impact on the guys. Keeping the eternal perspective in mind, more important than winning games was investing in the players' lives. Overall, it was a very positive and successful 2017-2018 season.

The other assistant coach was new to the school, too, and we became friends. The more we talked and got to know each other and shared our dreams, it became apparent that we had similar interests and aspirations. So, we discussed going into business together. We pursued starting a talent management group. We would facilitate athletes, actors, actresses, models, and musicians on their journey to success. We secured several clients quickly. We also started an AAU program. In addition, we accepted a position as recruiters for a local Christian university. These roles were all okay for a while, but God ended up closing those doors and steering me in a different direction.

As of now, I am writing this book and pursuing some other dreams of mine, and I don't know what God's ultimate plan is for my career, but I do know it is going to wonderful (*Jeremiah 29:11*).

One thing my grandma often reminds me of is that "I am the head and not the tail." So, I press on to what God has in store for me in the future. *Proverbs 16:9 says, "Man can make his plans, but it is God who orders his steps."*

Even though my life thus far hasn't gone exactly the way I had hoped, dreamed, or envisioned, I know God's ways are higher than my ways; therefore, I choose to continue to trust Him totally.

17

Lessons Learned

Given that division 1 basketball was a goal of mine, but it did not play out like I thought it would, what can I take away from the experience?

1. I learned a lot of valuable lessons.
2. I grew stronger as an individual.
3. My character was strengthened.
4. I learned very quickly that division 1 basketball is a business.
5. I learned that the basketball world is a small world; everybody knows everybody.
6. I made a lot of connections along the way.
7. There were positives to the overall experience.
8. There were also very real negatives that were, unfortunately, part of the experience.
9. I will always cherish the good memories.
10. I will always be grateful for the opportunity.
11. I choose to let go of the negative experiences and forgive those who offended me.

12. Playing a sport at the division 1 level is very time consuming, demanding, and hard work. It's like going to college and having a full-time job at the same time.
13. There are some "glamorous" aspects to the experience, but it is definitely not all glamour. There are moments you feel like a celebrity (signing autographs, being asked to have your picture taken with fans, getting recognized when you are out and about) and then there are moments when you feel used and taken advantage of.
14. Fans can be relentless. They are for you when you do well, not so much when you are struggling. You can't please everyone any of the time.
15. You have to be careful to ignore the negative comments on the internet. There is a very real mental aspect of the game that has to be kept in check.
16. Some athletes are naturally more confident than others. Confidence goes a long way to facilitate great performance. Typically, the more confident you are as an athlete, the better you perform.
17. I was expected to do a lot of things that were out of my comfort zone (speaking to crowds of donors, giving interviews, etc.) But it was

good for me to do those things I considered uncomfortable. It stretched me, but I gained confidence by doing it.
18. People disappoint. Whether it is due to the pressure of the "business" or for whatever reason, people may say unkind things to you and treat you poorly.
19. Given numerous injuries and surgeries, I had to persevere to keep coming back. Perseverance is key. Keep on keeping on!
20. At times, I had to refrain from complaining and feeling sorry for myself.
21. What helped me endure more than anything was my faith in God. I fully believe He has a purpose for each one of us. And my desire is to accomplish His plans and purpose for my life. My faith is stronger because of all God allowed me to walk through.
22. You have to choose to do what is right even when others around you aren't doing the same.
23. You have to choose to be respectful even when others aren't respectful.
24. I had to have the strength of character to live a different lifestyle and refrain from doing what the majority did.

25. The people you meet along life's journey, you meet for a reason. You can learn something from them. Maybe God wants to use you to be a light and positive influence on them. But for some reason, God ordained that your paths crossed.

Given all that I have witnessed and experienced, what do I do with all that I have learned? One thing I know is that I want to continue to give back. I want to be able to help younger guys and be an encouragement to anyone who is walking through a difficult experience. I choose to live differently than the majority and have learned along the way what I don't want to be like or emulate.

18

What Is It Really Like to be a College Athlete?

The Schedule

A typical day in the life of a college athlete: get up early, workout prior to class, attend classes, go to practice after class, lift weights, do conditioning exercises, spend extra time shooting, watch film, go to various athletic meetings, do homework, study for tests, participate in group projects, attend community events, speak at donor events, travel with the team to games, go to game day shootarounds, etc. There is always a lot going on. When you first arrive on campus, you soon realize that your schedule is no longer your own. You are told where to be and when. You don't receive much advance notice, and plans are often changed. Free time is nonexistent, and when you do rarely get some time to yourself, you are exhausted. It's a 7-days-a-week-12-hours-a-day job.

The Coaching Staff

The student-athlete's interaction with the coaching staff plays a vital role in the player's success. Coaches have an awesome opportunity and responsibility to mentor, be a good example, help the whole person for life. And yet so many coaches fall short due to the pressure of the business, the pressure to win games, egos, or feelings of importance. It's unfortunate when coaches miss the mark. What is really important in life is people, making a positive difference in another person's life, leaving an impact on the individual that they will never forget, all while instilling values and principles they can take with them in their future endeavors.

The sowing and reaping principle is a very real part of God's economy. What we sow, we will reap at some point. Sowing good seeds, we will, in turn, reap good seeds. Sowing kindness, we will be shown kindness in return. Treating others with respect, we will be respected. Valuing people and treating them accordingly, we will be valued, too. The Golden Rule applies as well. Do unto others as you would have others do unto you. Coaches should treat their players like they would want someone to treat their children.

The Locker Room

Most of what is said in the locker room should not be shared.

The Perks

Free athletic gear, charter plane rides, per diem money, free meals, academic support, television coverage, etc.

Team Dynamics

The people you are going to be around is the most important thing to consider when picking a school. All top-level division 1 schools are comparable in terms of every other aspect including facilities, practice routines, and overall programs, but because you do spend so much time with your teammates and coaches, you want to be sure their company is enjoyable. That can make or break the whole experience. Not to mention, the on-court or on-field component can determine your own personal success. If your team does not pass you the ball or your coach does not believe in you, it is going to be awfully hard to do well. It is nearly impossible to know what it is going to be like before going into it, so pray a lot and take your time with the decision to get the best possible idea of how it is going to go.

Positives vs Negatives

As with most life experiences, there are both positive and negative aspects of being a college athlete. To gain perspective, it can be helpful to see the comparisons side by side:

POSITIVES	NEGATIVES
• Picture Day • Banners raised • Free athletic apparel • Tournament gifts • Scholarship money • Gameday recognition • Charter plane rides • Going to famous arenas • Playing top teams • Per diem money • NIT Championship ring • NCAA Sweet 16 ring • Games at Madison Square Garden • Games at local venues: American Airlines Center and AT&T Stadium • Went to Hawaii and participated in the Maui Invitational, going all the way to the championship • Thanksgiving in Destin, Florida, for another tournament • Meeting President Donald Trump and countless other celebrity experiences	• Negative remarks on social media • Lack of or no communication from coaches • Being singled out in practices/yelled and cursed at • Coaches changing my shot • Required events (compliance meetings, etc.) • School + workouts + film • Long days • Injuries • Surgeries and treatments

Current President of the United States Donald Trump.

Practice at University of Kansas' Allen Fieldhouse, where three friends and former teammates now currently play and I visit regularly: Elijah Elliott, Dedric Lawson, and KJ Lawson.

Practice at Madison Square Garden in the Knicks locker room, where two friends and former TAPPS hoopers currently play: Emmanuel Mudiay and Luke Kornet.

Maui Invitational with Jonathan Motley and John Heard.

Players entrance at former school (former teammates and friends previously unmentioned: AJ Walton, professional basketball; Jacob Neubert, businessman; LJ Rose, professional basketball; Deuce Bello, professional basketball; Brady Heslip, professional basketball).

With Alex Moffatt, best player to ever come out of Somerville, TN.

AT&T Stadium, home of the Dallas Cowboys (for a game against Kentucky).

19

Growth from Freshman Year to Senior Year

- Public speaking
- Teamwork/relating to people
- Job of basketball and school (time management, responsibility, deadlines, travel)
- Overall maturity
- Freshman season is your first time to do everything; after the first year, the whole process is a less difficult transition.
- The longer you are there the stronger you get, the more skills you develop, and the better you become as a player overall.

There are tremendous growth opportunities throughout college, and most people grow up a lot. Student-athletes tend to grow up even more by balancing high-level college athletics combined with a normal school routine. You spend almost your whole life, from the time you are a freshman in high school to the time your college career is over, focused on your athletic performance. You do not experience normal life and miss out on a lot of things that most sixteen to twenty-four-year-olds get to experience.

Many times, you think that it is not worth it and want to be a regular student. However, I have lived both sides of the coin and have come to realize that being a regular student is not all that it is cracked up to be. If you can get a free college education, better yourself in a countless number of ways, and increase your resume by being a student-athlete, it is definitely worth all the hardship that comes along with it. You'll have plenty of time afterward to catch up on whatever you missed out on.

20

When it Comes to an End

The end of an era… Life as you've known it for years… From life revolving around basketball to not… What now?

I always thought that I wanted to be in the NBA, and as I got older, that dream looked like it could very well become a reality. However, that was not God's plan for me, at least at that time. Now I have to adjust and move on, open and ready for whatever He has for me. I know that His plan is better than anything I could possibly imagine, and I just have to make sure I follow the plan accordingly. I have tried to pursue a professional basketball career overseas, but so far it has not worked out, and that is okay. Maybe I will play professionally after this book, or maybe I won't, but I want to do whatever God wants me to do.

It has been a big adjustment in the last couple of years not playing on a real team, but I have had some other experiences that have been good for me. Sometimes the enemy tries to tell you that you are not good enough, you have been a failure, and it was all for nothing, but I don't receive that. I have spent much time learning what I like to do and what I don't and have experimented with various different careers.

People in your life change and start acting differently toward you when you are not doing something they deem important. I have come to realize that in life there are three types of friends: real friends, convenience friends, and fake friends. I've experienced all three types after leaving my first college team and again after I left the team at my second university. You are not as well liked all the sudden, and you see who is real and who is not. Friends come and go, some stick with you, and then others are clearly just your "friend" when they think you might be famous one day.

I don't have a problem with this situation anymore like I used to, because I have learned how the world works. I see things more clearly, and I understand better whom to associate with and whom not to. I know that my recognition needs to come from God and God alone because people are not perfect and will always disappoint. But with God, He is perfect and will never disappoint.

I still believe that God has big plans for me to do big things in the near future, and I know He will work it all out for me. Until then and for the rest of my life, I will simply choose to follow Him and let Him guide the way and direct my path.

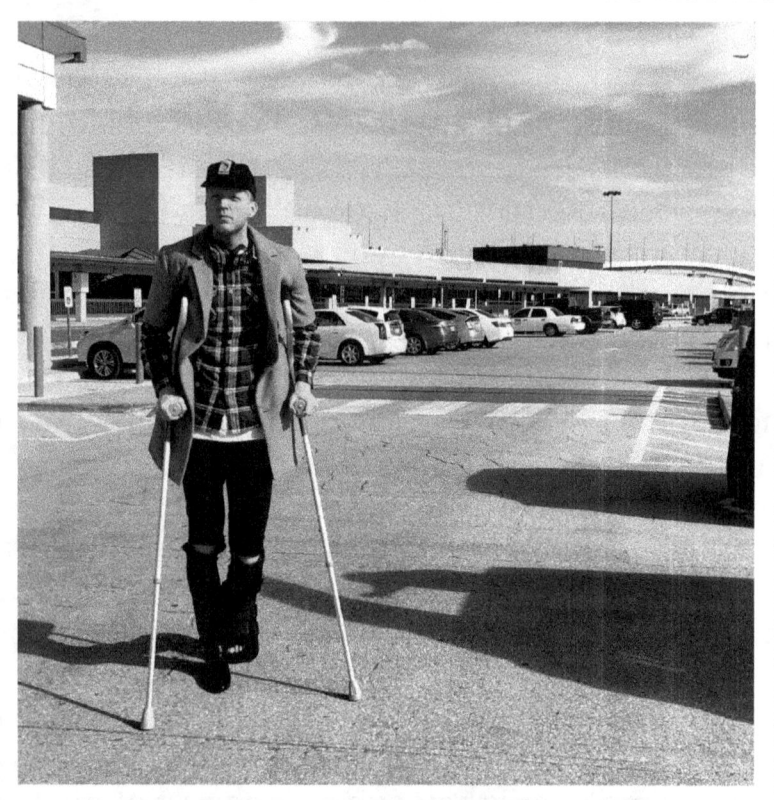

Family

How can I use what I have learned to help others and give back?
1. Learn from my negative experiences and determine to do differently.
2. Share what I have learned in hopes that it will help someone else on their journey.
3. Coach
4. Teach
5. Train
6. Help others in the recruiting process
7. Be an encourager, making others feel valued and important
8. Use my blessings to be a blessing

One student at my alma mater wrote a paper on me as his hero. Even recently, someone reached out to me saying that their son wanted to be just like me when he got older. You have more of an impact on others than you realize. You never know who is watching you, looking for a role model, or simply someone to look up to.

Spending time with local elementary school children.

My Hero

My hero is Chad Rykhoek. Ever since he started to play on the FWC Varsity team I have admired him and looked up to him. When I grow up I want to play basketball as good as him. I always love to watch him play basketball. I can't wait till next basketball season to see him play for the Baylor Bears. He is so awesome, I wish I could be him. Although I can't be him, I will always try to reflect him.

21

The Mental Aspect

The mental aspect of being a college athlete is a crucial component. The importance of mental toughness cannot be overemphasized.

Some insights I discovered along the way include:

- Handle attacks with courage and dignity.
- Stand strong against the enemy's flaming arrows.
- Resist temptations.
- Don't doubt yourself.
- Know who you are in Christ.
- Stay positive. Look at the glass as half full.
- Take one day at a time.
- Determine to overcome and persevere through all obstacles.
- Ask God daily to control your thoughts and take captive any thoughts that are not from Him.
- Ignore the haters. Everyone has different opinions. They cannot truly know what it is like to be you if they haven't walked in your shoes.

22

The Medical Aspect

I was healthy my entire life up until college. I rarely went to the doctor, had no broken bones, and no serious illnesses or procedures. This all changed dramatically over the course of my college career. After becoming a scholarship athlete, I experienced:

- Countless doctor visits
- Seven surgeries and procedures over three years, which included pre-op procedures, anesthesia, side effects of anesthesia, pain meds, ice sessions for days, redressing bandages, stitches, crutches or a boot, post-op appointments, rehab to regain strength, and conditioning when cleared to resume normal activity. Out-of-town surgeries were particularly challenging, trying to recover in a hotel for a day post-surgery and then heading to the airport on crutches and pain meds to catch a flight home.
- Multiple physical therapy sessions for months at a time
- Chiropractor appointments
- Stretching appointments
- Massages
- Targeted muscle treatments
- Acupuncture

- Prescribed steroid injections to promote healing
- Shingles
- Kidney stones
- Chronic TMJ
- Stem cell injections

23

In Retrospect

Would I change anything? Would I do anything differently? Given the information I had at the time, I made the best decisions I could. So, if God allowed things to happen that were not a part of my plan, then I just have to walk through it with Him, trusting Him to help me every step of the way. His ways and thoughts are higher than ours. His plan is perfect. We will understand more clearly the answer to all the whys one of these days.

In a phone conversation in the beginning of my freshman year when I was very down, my mom asked me to share something positive, and I really could not think of one positive thing to share. And when I was at one of my lowest points, my mom said that God was building a testimony in my life, a story that I could share on down the road, a "look what God did" story. That gave me purpose and reassured me that all of this would be worth it and work out for my good somehow, someday.

24

Regrets?

Although I do have a few small regrets, overall, I am glad everything happened just the way that it did. I was never a bad kid and have been a Christian since a young age, but I was not fully dedicated to that lifestyle until everything came crashing down. It was at my lowest point when I realized that I could not do everything by myself. In fact, I needed God for everything. He humbled me and took basketball away so that I could rededicate my life to Him. I went from living in the world at times while also living in the Christian circle, to going all the way in and trying to live for Jesus and be a good example at all times.

I remember when I was having an issue with kidney stones at my apartment by myself, alone, and very lonely in Waco, Texas. It was the worst pain I had experienced in my life up to that point, and I literally felt like I was maybe going to die. I cried out to God and realized all the bad ways in which I had been acting. I had put God to the side and was living my life trying to do things my own way. Everything in my life up until college had gone pretty smoothly, and I took my focus off God and took for granted everything that He had given me. I was ungrateful, sad, and acting out in ways that were not typical behavior for me. I isolated myself and was in a tough place. After a few moments though, when I was in my room, I felt like I completely turned my life around. All the bad times I had experienced throughout college culminated here, and I surrendered completely to Him. I ended up having to drive myself to the emergency room and was in excruciating pain. The kidney stones subsided after a week or so of recovery, and I decided to do things differently.

    God placed a friend in my life who got me going to church again with a student ministry group that hosted service once a week on campus. This was my senior year of college and some of the first times I had gone to church in that city. I was so upset and consumed with myself all the years before, I didn't want to associate with anything or anyone in that town. Since graduating, I have steadily gotten closer to God and grown in my Christianity and devotion to Him. I feel as though if all of these bad things had not happened to me and instead life had been a straight road that led to the NBA, my relationship with Jesus would not have been nearly as good as it needed to be. Therefore, I look back and understand that everything truly does happen for a reason, and I see how everything actually came together for my good.

    From a worldly perspective, it may seem as though I failed, but I actually succeeded, because I grew close to God, our Creator, and am on the right path for the rest of eternity. He gave me a testimony that can hopefully bring light to others going through similar situations.

25

Different Personality Types

My personality is one that is hesitant. I can be quite shy around people I do not know and can be less than confident until I feel comfortable in my surroundings. Basketball is fully reliant on confidence, as is life. Often, I let other people influence my confidence and bring me down. I let myself concentrate too much on other people's opinions of me rather than believing and focusing on what God thinks about me. People are important, and you need to surround yourself with others who are going to build you up, not tear you down.

If you are trying to go to the NBA, or if you are trying to make it to the top level of a business, it is frequently all about being in the right place at the right time. The people who have connections and value every relationship will typically go a lot farther than those who try to live life solo. It is important to be secure in yourself and secure in God, knowing that you can do anything that He has planned for your life.

We all have a purpose, and the sooner you understand what that purpose is, the better. God is with you and has great plans for you; you just have to surrender your will to Him, submit to His ways, and not think that you alone are enough. You are never enough without God. He owns the entire universe, and everything you have comes from Him.

There is a fine line between confidence and arrogance, but when you spend time with God, studying the Bible, praying, worshiping, etc., you will be able to discern the difference. I am glad that I was typically one to think before I spoke, but sometimes it would have been more beneficial for me to stand up for myself and let people know how I really felt. Being upfront and communicating with others honestly and with transparency is a great way to go through life. Regardless of what you have done up to this point, God is still with you and you can turn your life around instantly just by giving yourself fully over to Him.

26

Advice for Young Athletes

- Work hard
- Be discerning
- Do your research
- Pray
- Follow your heart
- Persevere
- Never give up
- Always remember your purpose
- Keep in mind that you are building your story, and you can use your story to help someone else on down the road.
- Do not conform to the world's ways
- Stand strong
- Live with good character
- Maintain your integrity

Conclusion

Life can be compared to a puzzle. After we are born, we add to the puzzle piece by piece as we walk through our every day. When God calls us home, we will look back at the completed puzzle titled "My Life", and it will all make sense. God, in His infinite wisdom, orchestrated your life's events, allowing certain things to happen or not, to complete His perfect plan for you. My story is not exactly like anyone else's. But hopefully, others can relate to parts of my journey and take away courage, encouragement, hope, and motivation to help them live out their own story.

May God bless you on your life journey.

"The Lord bless you and keep you; the Lord make His face shine on you and be gracious to you; the Lord turn His face toward you and give you peace."
(Numbers 6:24-26)

www.ingramcontent.com/pod-product-compliance
Lightning Source LLC
Chambersburg PA
CBHW070204100426
42743CB00013B/3038